The MAILBOX®

The Education Center®

For Every Learner™

grade 1

Phonics

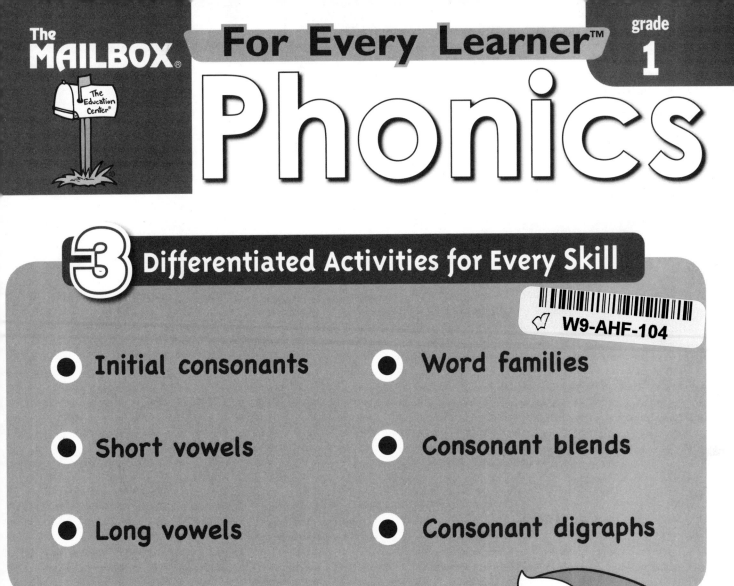

3 Differentiated Activities for Every Skill

W9-AHF-104

- Initial consonants
- Short vowels
- Long vowels
- Word families
- Consonant blends
- Consonant digraphs

Covers 19 key skills!

Editorial Team: Becky S. Andrews, Diane Badden, Kimberley Bruck, Karen A. Brudnak, Kitty Campbell, Jenny Chapman, Pam Crane, Chris Curry, Lynette Dickerson, Lynn Drolet, Sarah Foreman, Tazmen Hansen, Marsha Heim, Lori Z. Henry, Angela Kamstra-Jacobson, Debra Liverman, Dorothy C. McKinney, Thad H. McLaurin, Sharon Murphy, Jennifer Nunn, Gerri Primak, Mark Rainey, Greg D. Rieves, Kelly Robertson, Hope Rodgers, Rebecca Saunders, Donna K. Teal, Joshua Thomas

www.themailbox.com

©2009 The Mailbox® Books
All rights reserved.
ISBN10 #1-56234-863-9 • ISBN13 #978-156234-863-2

Manufactured in the United States
10 9 8 7 6 5 4 3 2 1

Table of Contents

Practice each skill **3** different ways!

What's Inside

Inspectors at Work

Initial consonants: *c, h, n, p*

(Pages 13 and 14)
1. Cut out the cards.
2. Sort the cards by beginning letter.
3. Glue each set next to the matching letter on your other page.

Inspectors at Work

Initial consonants: *c, h, n, p*

Name

c

h

n

p

14

Formats and levels of difficulty vary!

Keeping Track

Initial consonants: *c, h, n, p*

Name

1. Spin the spinner.
2. If the letter spun is the beginning letter of picture 1, color the picture. If it is not, spin again.
3. Repeat Step 2 until each picture is colored in order.

c   h

n   p

15

Which Way?

Initial consonants: *c, h, n, p*

Name

Color the pawprint with the beginning letter for each picture.
Write the word on the matching line.

1. _____
2. _____
3. _____
4. _____
5. _____
6. _____
7. _____
8. _____

16

Choose the right practice for each learner!

For Every Learner™: Phonics • ©The Mailbox® Books • TEC61185   3

Skills Checklist

Assessment Code
M = More practice needed
S = Successful

Skills	Practice 1	Practice 2	Practice 3	Notes
Initial consonants: *b, m, r*				
Initial consonants: *g, s, t*				
Initial consonants: *c, h, n, p*				
Initial consonants: *d, f, j, k, l*				
Short vowels: *a, i*				
Short vowels: *e, o*				
Short vowels: *a, u*				
Short vowels: *a, e, i, o, u*				
Long vowels: *a, i*				
Long vowels: *e, o, u*				
Long vowels: *a, e, i, o, u*				
Short and long vowels: *a, e, i, o, u*				
Word families: *-an, -ap, -at*				
Word families: *-ell, -et, -ock, -og*				
Word families: *-an, -en, -in, -un*				
Word families: *-ail, -ain, -ake*				
Word families: *-eat, -ight, -oat*				
Consonant blends: *sk, sm, sp, st*				
Consonant digraphs: *ch, sh, th, wh*				

For Every Learner™: Phonics • ©The Mailbox® Books • TEC61185

Note to the teacher: To track the skill progress of individual students, personalize copies of the page. Each time a student completes a practice page, use the provided code to note an assessment of his work.

Cozy Koala

(Pages 5 and 6)

1. Cut out the cards below.
2. Name the picture on each card.
3. Glue each card to match the beginning letter on your other page.

For Every Learner™: Phonics • ©The Mailbox® Books • TEC61185

Name

Cozy Koala

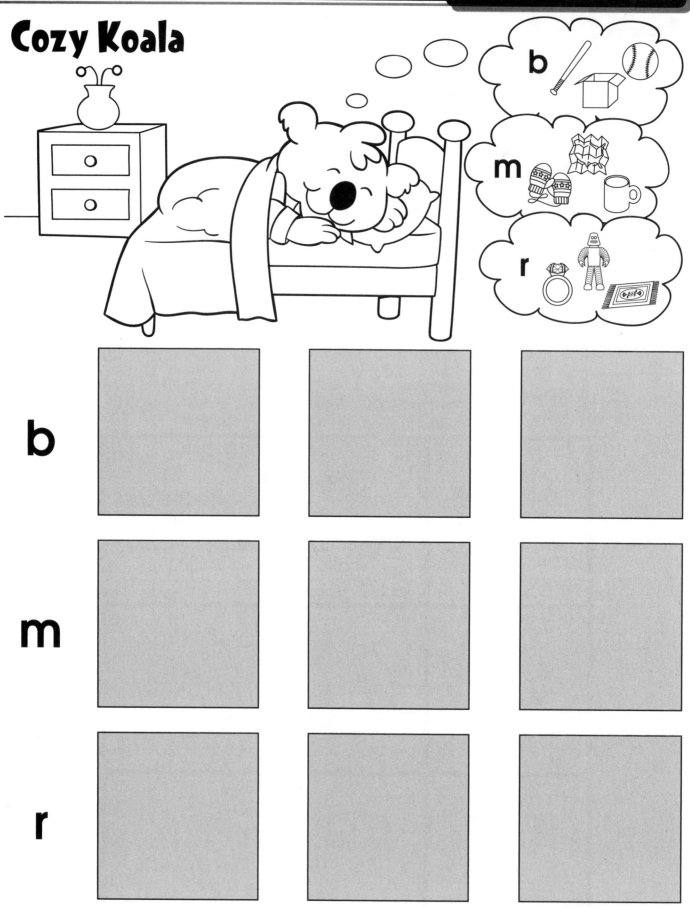

b

m

r

So Sleepy!

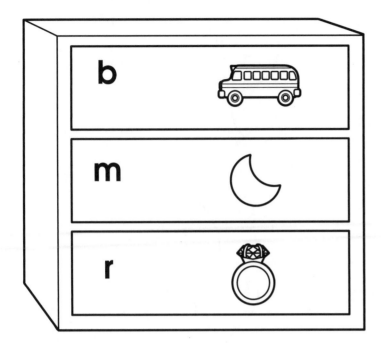

Write **b**, **m**, or **r**.

 ___ag

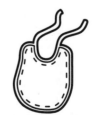 ___an

 ___ock

 ___ug

 ___op

 ___at

 ___ap

 ___ib

Bedtime Books

1. Write the beginning letter for each picture below.
2. Cut out the cards.
3. Sort the cards by beginning letter.
4. On another sheet of paper, glue each set in a separate row.

For Every Learner™: Phonics • ©The Mailbox® Books • TEC61185

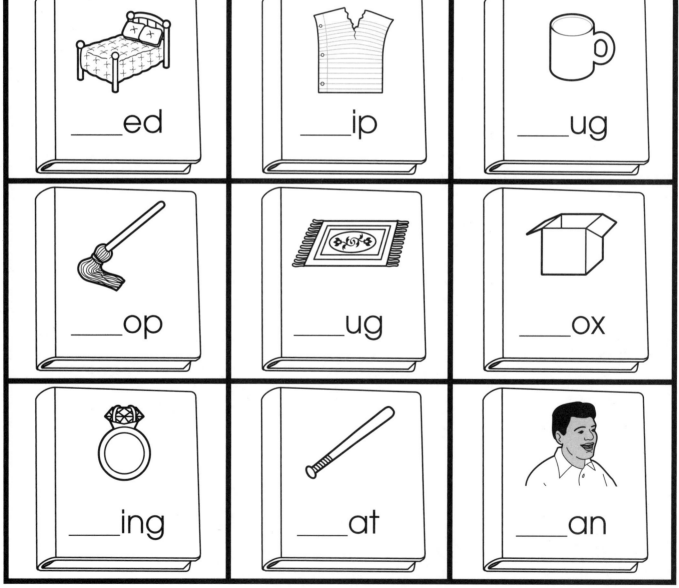

___ed

___ip

___ug

___op

___ug

___ox

___ing

___at

___an

Name

Bags of Birdseed

Name each picture.
Say the beginning sound.
Write the letter.

tub

___en

___urkey

___urtle

sun

___ad

___ock

___eal

game

___um

___irl

___oat

For Every Learner™: *Phonics* • ©The Mailbox® Books • TEC61185

9

To the Birdbath!

Directions for two players:

1. Put your game markers on START.
2. In turn, roll a die and move your marker.
3. Name the picture you land on and write its beginning letter on the line. If the letter is already written, go back to your previous space and roll again.
4. The first player to reach FINISH wins!

START

Miss one turn.

FINISH

Find That Home!

(Pages 11 and 12)

1. Cut out the cards below.
2. Sort the cards by beginning letter.
3. Glue each set to a birdhouse on your other page.
4. Write the beginning letter at the top of each birdhouse.

For Every Learner™: Phonics • ©The Mailbox® Books • TEC61185

Name

Find That Home!

12

Initial consonants: *g, s, t*

For Every Learner™: Phonics • ©The Mailbox® Books • TEC61185

Note to the teacher: Use with "Find That Home!" on page 11.

Inspectors at Work

(Pages 13 and 14)

1. Cut out the cards.
2. Sort the cards by beginning letter.
3. Glue each set next to the matching letter on your other page.

For Every Learner™: Phonics • ©The Mailbox® Books • TEC61185

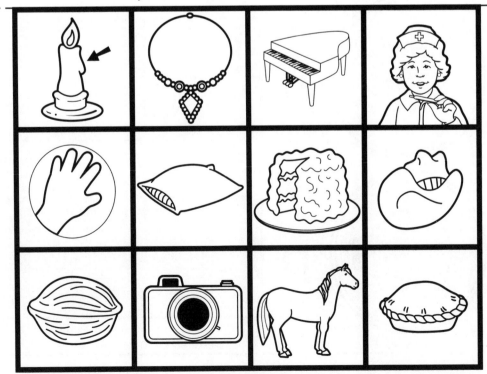

Inspectors at Work

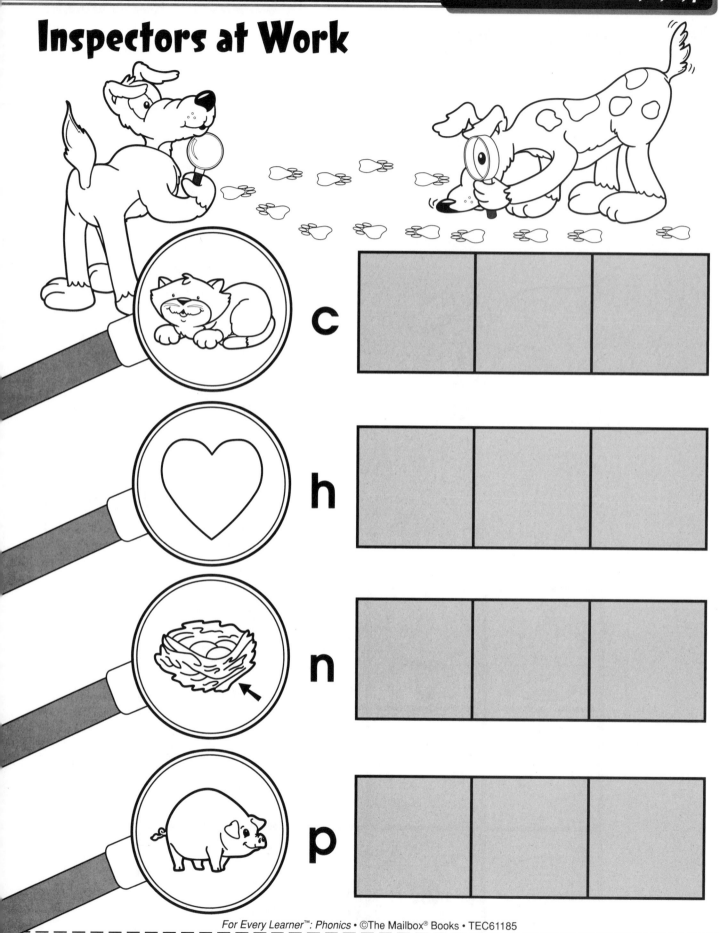

c

h

n

p

For Every Learner™: Phonics • ©The Mailbox® Books • TEC61185

14   **Note to the teacher:** Use with "Inspectors at Work" on page 13.

Keeping Track

1. Spin the spinner.
2. If the letter spun is the beginning letter of picture 1, color the picture. If it is not, spin again.
3. Repeat Step 2 until each picture is colored in order.

Which Way?

Color the pawprint with the beginning letter for each picture.
Write the word on the matching line.

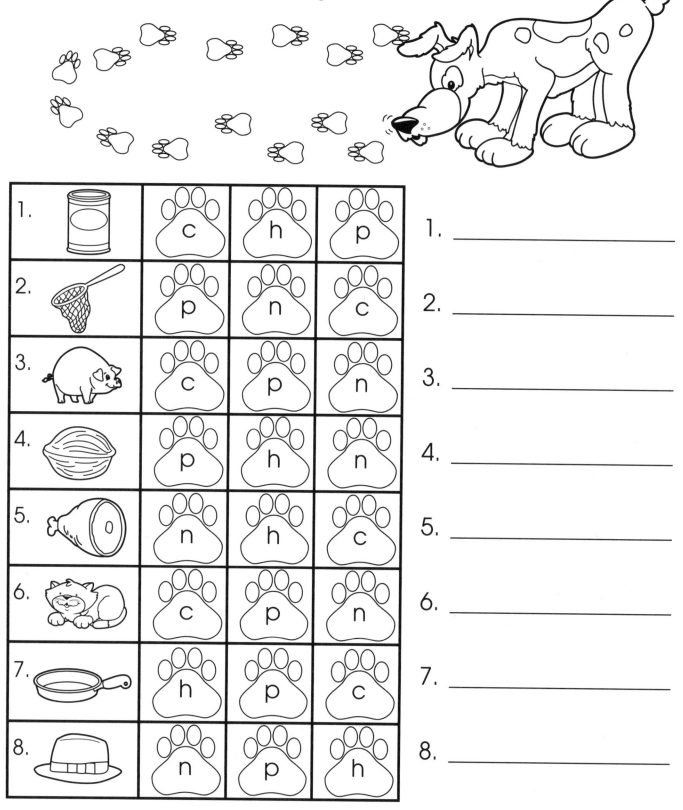

1. _____

2. _____

3. _____

4. _____

5. _____

6. _____

7. _____

8. _____

For Every Learner™: Phonics • ©The Mailbox® Books • TEC61185

Monster Match
(Pages 17 and 18)

1. Cut out the cards.
2. Sort the cards by beginning letter.
3. Glue each set below the matching monster on your other page.

For Every Learner™: Phonics • ©The Mailbox® Books • TEC61185

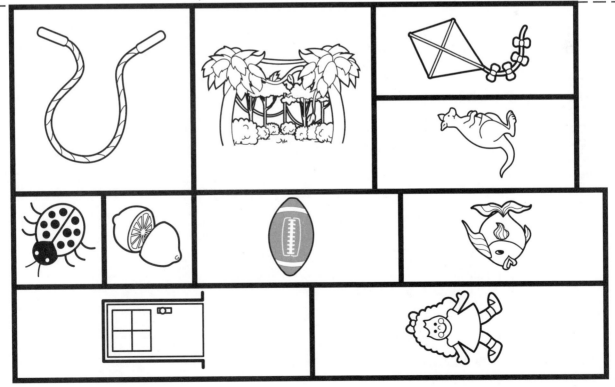

Initial consonants: *d, f, j, k, l*

Monster Match

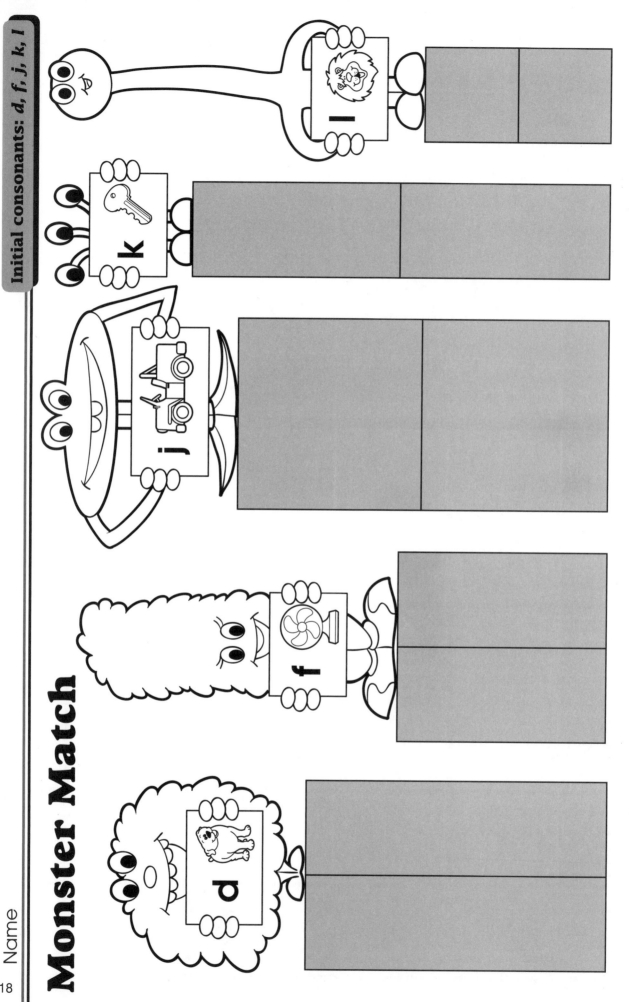

For Every Learner™: Phonics • ©The Mailbox® Books • TEC61185

Note to the teacher: Use with "Monster Match" on page 17.

Name

Monster Mush

Write the beginning letter for each picture.
Color a matching bowl for each letter you write.

Monster Sightings!

1. Write the missing letter on each strip below.
2. Read each sentence.
3. Cut out the sentence strips.
4. Staple the strips together to make a booklet.

For Every Learner™: Phonics • ©The Mailbox® Books • TEC61185

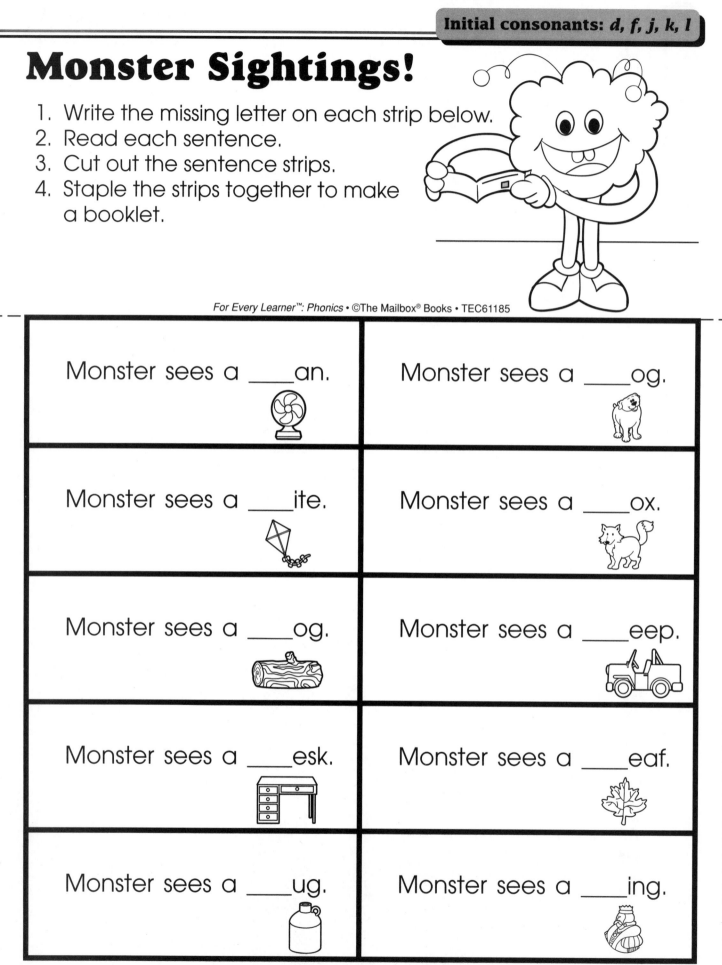

Monster sees a ____an.

Monster sees a ____og.

Monster sees a ____ite.

Monster sees a ____ox.

Monster sees a ____og.

Monster sees a ____eep.

Monster sees a ____esk.

Monster sees a ____eaf.

Monster sees a ____ug.

Monster sees a ____ing.

Feeding the Fish

Color by the code.

Color Code

a as in  —blue

i as in —green

bat

six

hat

kick

lip

wig

flag

fan

pin

pan

Best Friends

1. Write **a** or **i** to complete each word.
2. Cut out the cards.
3. Sort the cards by vowel.
4. On another sheet of paper, glue each set of cards under the matching fishbowl card.

For Every Learner™: Phonics • ©The Mailbox® Books • TEC61185

a as in

i as in

m__p

b__b

p__g

h__m

c__n

b__t

s__x

p__n

Name _____

Funny Faces
(Pages 23 and 24)

1. Cut out the puzzle pieces on your other page.
2. Name each picture and write the word.
3. Sort the pieces by vowel.
4. Glue each set on the matching square to make a puzzle.

short i

short a

Funny Faces

For Every Learner™: Phonics • ©The Mailbox® Books • TEC61185

Note to the teacher: Use with "Funny Faces" on page 23.

A Big Spill
(Pages 25 and 26)

1. Cut out the cards.
2. Sort the cards by vowel.
3. Glue each set in the matching row on your other page.

For Every Learner™: Phonics • ©The Mailbox® Books • TEC61185

| s**o**ck | p**o**t | b**e**ll | f**o**x |
| w**e**b | b**e**d | l**o**ck | t**e**n |

26 Name

A Big Spill

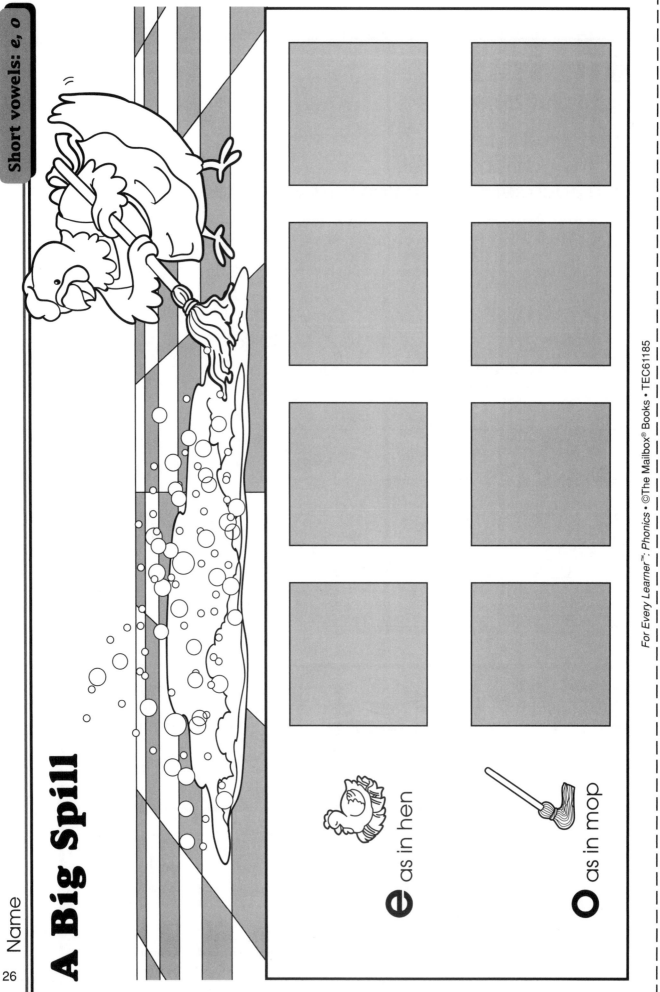

e as in hen

o as in mop

Note to the teacher: Use with "A Big Spill" on page 25.

Missing Mop

Color the space red if the vowel sounds like 🐔.

Color the space yellow if the vowel sounds like 🧹.

Circle.

What color was the path that led to the mop?   red   yellow

Super Suds

Write **e** or **o**.

f ___ x

l ___ ck

p ___ n

w ___ b

n ___ st

s ___ ck

Write each word from above in the matching sentence.

1. The spider made a _____.

2. The _____ has blue ink.

3. The bird built a _____.

4. I am wearing a _____ on each foot.

5. _____ the door when you leave.

6. The _____ has a big tail.

   For Every Learner™: Phonics • ©The Mailbox® Books • TEC61185

Name _____

Where Is the Park?

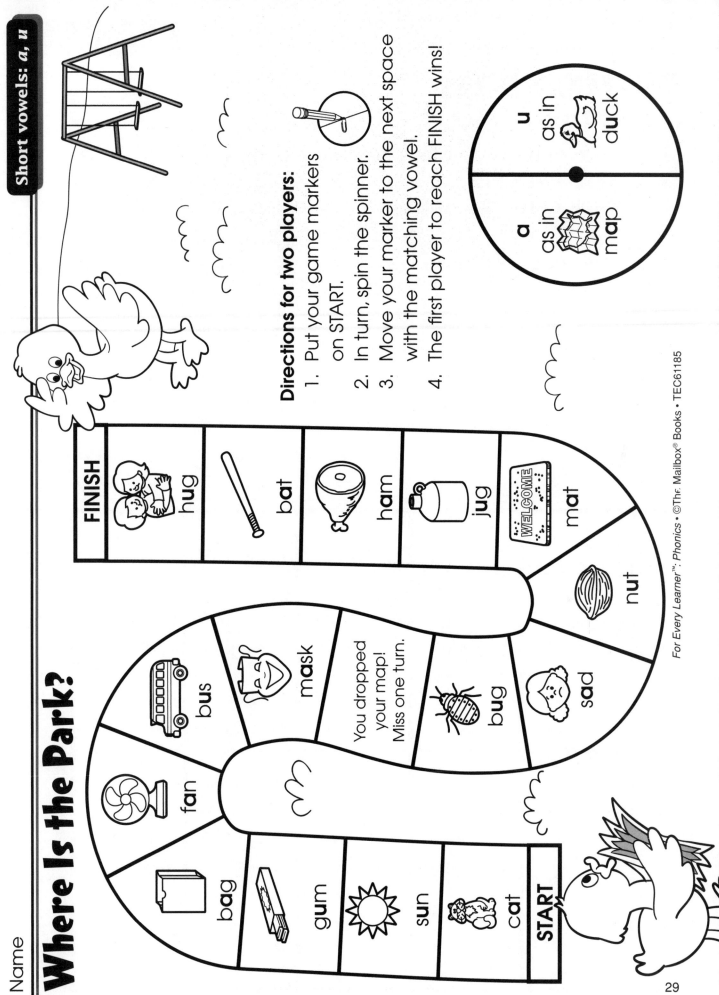

Directions for two players:

1. Put your game markers on START.
2. In turn, spin the spinner.
3. Move your marker to the next space with the matching vowel.
4. The first player to reach FINISH wins!

a	u
as in	as in
map	duck

FINISH

hug

bat

ham

jug

mat

nut

bus

mask

You dropped your map! Miss one turn.

bug

sad

fan

bag

gum

sun

cat

START

For Every Learner™: Phonics • ©The Mailbox® Books • TEC61185

Too Many Maps
(Pages 30 and 31)

1. Write **a** or **u** to complete each word below.
2. Cut out the cards.
3. Sort the cards by vowels.
4. Glue each set to the matching row on your other page.

For Every Learner™: Phonics • ©The Mailbox® Books • TEC61185

p___n	b___g	s___n	h___m	n___t
b___t	m___n	b___s	g___m	c___t

Name _____

Too Many Maps

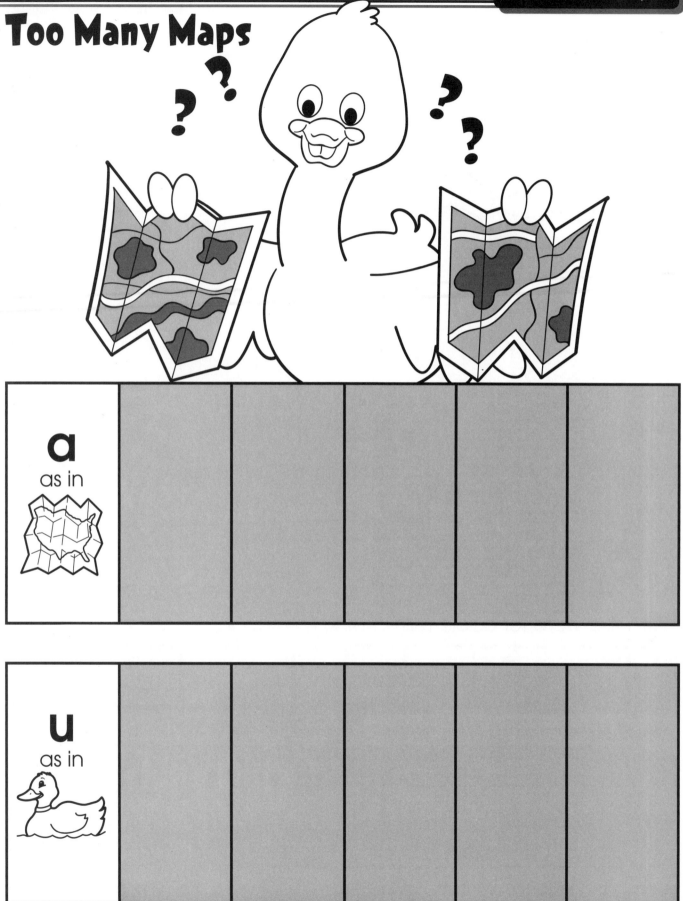

a as in					

u as in					

For Every Learner™: Phonics • ©The Mailbox® Books • TEC61185

Note to the teacher: Use with "Too Many Maps" on page 30.

31

Name

At the Park

Color by the code.

Color Code
a—brown
u—yellow

Write the word for each item in the picture.

a	u

Name

Up, Up, and Away!

Write the vowel.
Color a matching balloon.

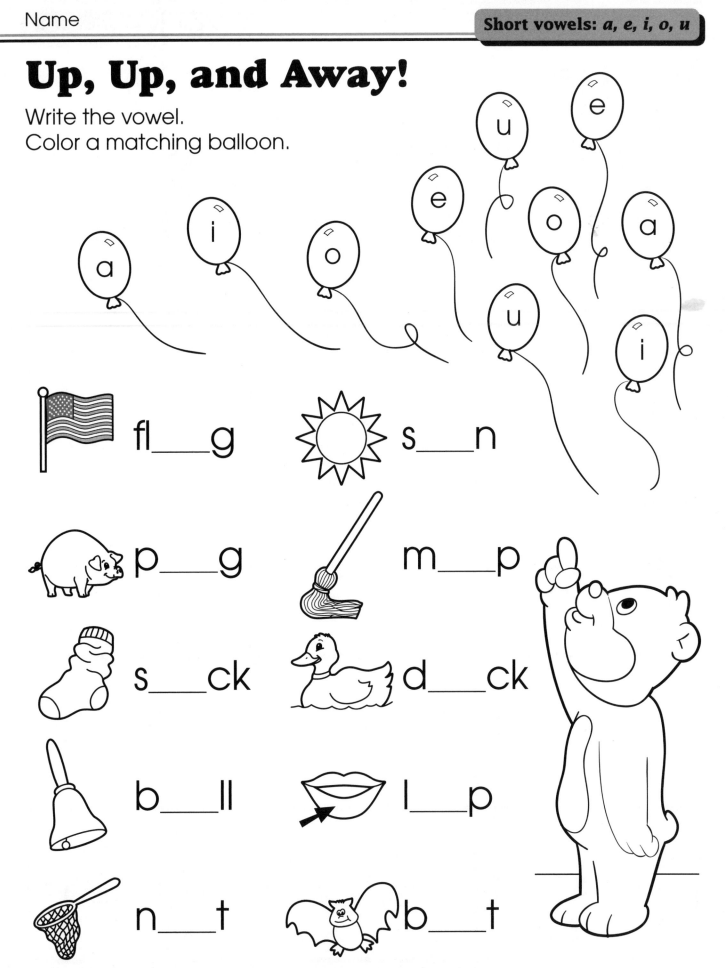

fl__g

s__n

p__g

m__p

s__ck

d__ck

b__ll

l__p

n__t

b__t

Hold On!

(Pages 34 and 35)

1. Write the short vowel to complete each word below.
2. Cut out the cards.
3. Take a card. Find a balloon on your other page with the matching vowel.
4. Write the word on the balloon.
5. Repeat Steps 3 and 4 for each card.

For Every Learner™: Phonics • ©The Mailbox® Books • TEC61185

p__t   p__g   c__ _n

n__t   g__m   m__p

c__t   d__g   b__b

s__n   b__d   m__n

Name

Hold On!

Note to the teacher: Use with "Hold On!" on page 34.

A Big Bunch

1. Write the missing short vowel so the sentence makes sense.
2. Cut out the strips and cards.
3. Match each sentence to its picture.
4. Glue each pair together on another sheet of paper.

For Every Learner™: *Phonics* • ©The Mailbox® Books • TEC61185

The p___g is in the mud.	A h___t is on my head.
The p___t is on the stove.	I ride a b___s.
A n___st is in a tree.	The c___t plays with yarn.

Sorting Laundry

(Pages 37–38)

1. Cut out the cards below.
2. Sort the cards by vowel sound.
3. Glue each set to the matching basket on your other page.

For Every Learner™: Phonics • ©The Mailbox® Books • TEC61185

Name _____

Sorting Laundry

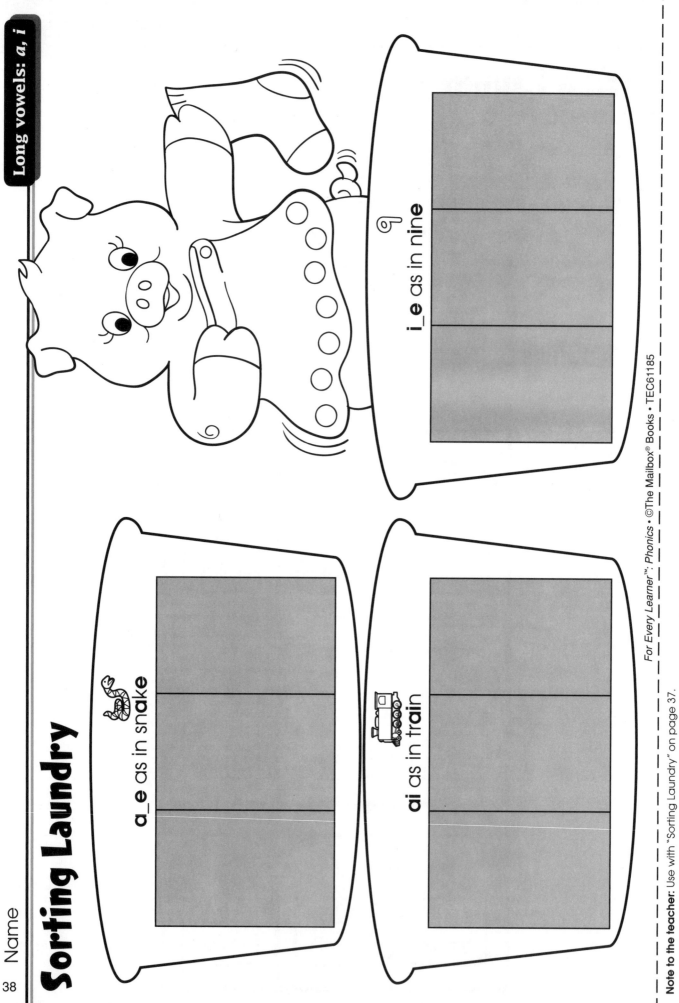

a_e as in snake

i_e as in nine

ai as in train

For Every Learner™: Phonics • ©The Mailbox® Books • TEC61185

Note to the teacher: Use with "Sorting Laundry" on page 37.

Name

Bubble Trouble

1. Write each word. Use the word bank.
2. Roll a die. Look at the color code. Color a bubble with a matching vowel spelling.
3. Repeat Step 2 until all the bubbles are colored.

Word Bank

tail	vase
bike	nail
kite	cage
rain	nine
rake	

Color Code

1 or 2 (blue)—**ai** as in m**ai**l
3 or 4 (yellow)—**a_e** as in g**a**m**e**
5 or 6 (green)—**i_e** as in m**i**c**e**

Time to Dry

Color by the code.

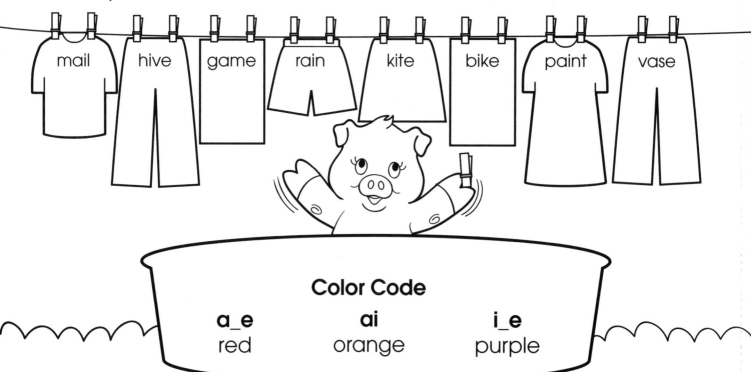

Color Code

a_e	**ai**	**i_e**
red	orange	purple

Complete each sentence with a word from above.

1. We came in to get out of the _____.

2. I like to ride my _____.

3. My friend sent me a card in the _____.

4. The _____ was full of bees.

5. What color did you _____ the box?

6. Tag is a fun _____.

7. She put the flowers in a _____.

8. I flew a _____ on a windy day.

   For Every Learner™: Phonics • ©The Mailbox® Books • TEC61185

Mice at the Movies

Color each ticket by the code.

bee

cone

feet

cube

tree

rose

note

wheel

mule

Color Code

ee—green

o_e—orange

u_e—blue

Movie Treats

1. Cut out the cards.
2. Glue the popcorn cartons along the bottom of another sheet of paper.
3. Sort the popcorn cards by vowel sounds.
4. Glue each set above the matching carton.

For Every Learner™: Phonics • ©The Mailbox® Books • TEC61185

A Funny Movie

(Pages 43 and 44)

1. Cut out the letter cards.
2. Name the first picture on your other page. Use the letter cards to spell the word.
3. Write each letter in the matching box. Then write the word on the line.
4. Circle the vowel spelling.
5. Repeat Steps 2 to 4 for each picture.

HA! HA! HA! HA!

e	e	e	o	u
b	c	f	h	l
m	n	r	s	t

A Funny Movie

Write each numbered letter from above on its matching line below.

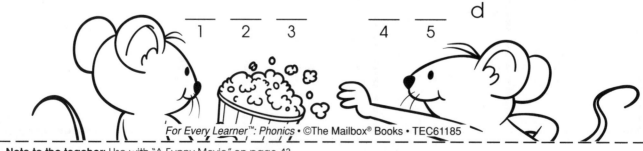

For Every Learner™: Phonics • ©The Mailbox® Books • TEC61185

44   **Note to the teacher:** Use with "A Funny Movie" on page 43.

Monkey Masterpiece

1. Spin the spinner.
2. Color a box with a matching vowel sound.
3. Repeat Step 2 until all the spaces are colored.

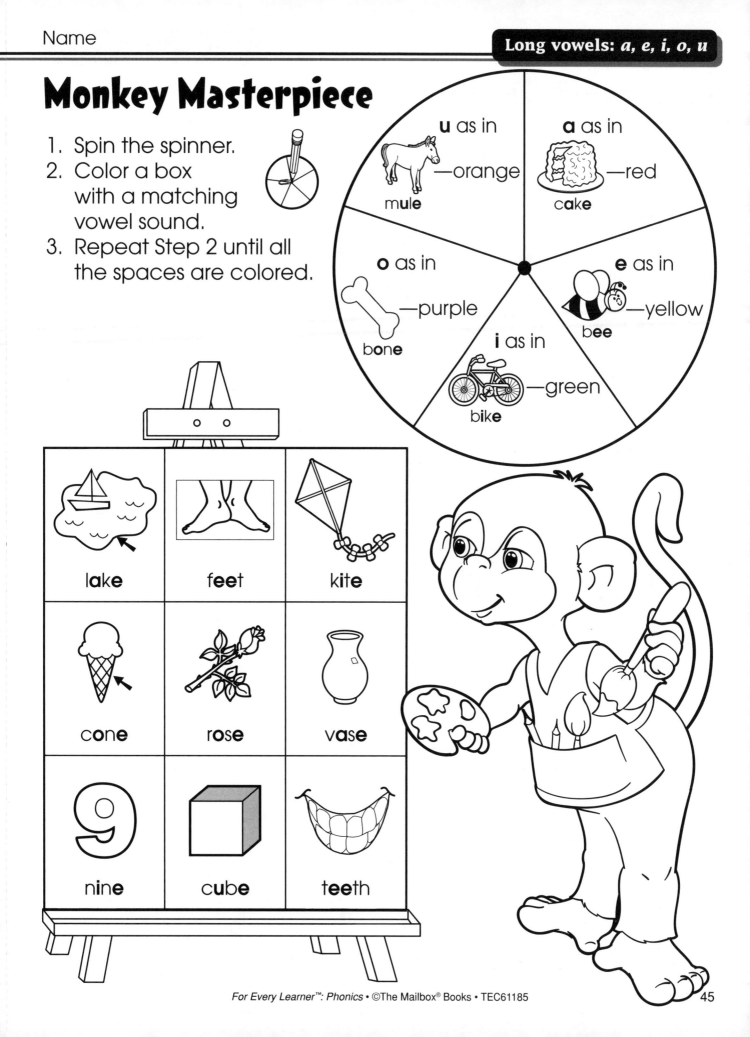

u as in
m**u**le —orange

a as in
c**a**ke —red

o as in
b**o**ne —purple

e as in
b**ee** —yellow

i as in
b**i**ke —green

lake	feet	kite
cone	rose	vase
nine	cube	teeth

Name

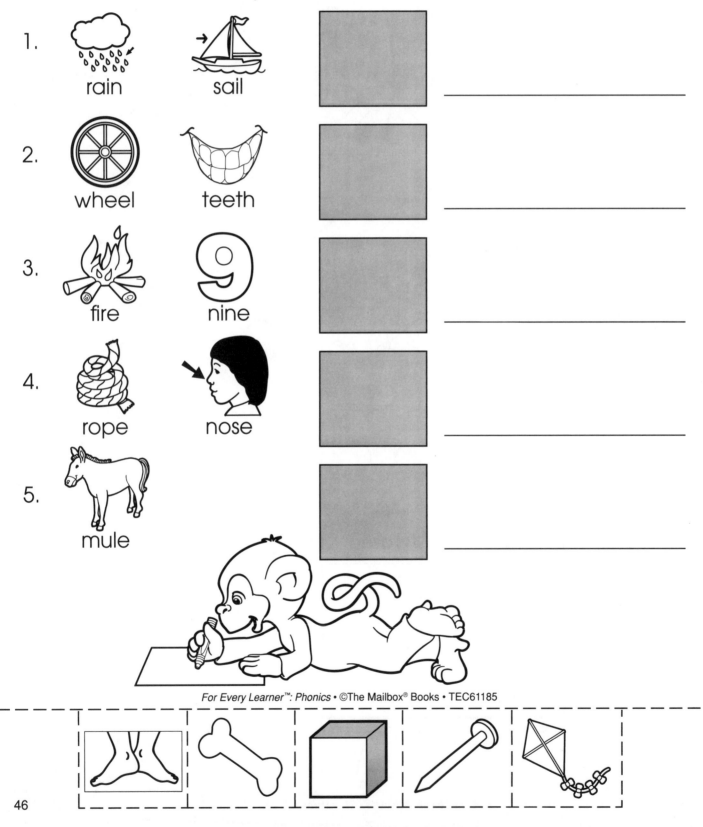

Creative Coloring

Cut.
Glue to match each vowel sound.
Write the word for each picture.

1. rain   sail

2. wheel   teeth

3. fire   nine

4. rope   nose

5. mule

For Every Learner™: Phonics • ©The Mailbox® Books • TEC61185

Plenty to Paint

(Pages 47 and 48)

1. Cut out the cards.
2. Sort the cards by vowel sound.
3. Glue each set in the matching column on your other page.
4. Write the word for each picture. (Hint: Each vowel spelling is used once.)

For Every Learner™: Phonics • ©The Mailbox® Books • TEC61185

Name

Plenty to Paint

Long a
a_e, ai, ay

Long e
ee, ea, ey

Long i
i_e, igh, ie

Long o
o_e, oa, ow

Long u
u_e, oe

48

Note to the teacher: Use with "Plenty to Paint" on page 47.

Name _____

Under the Big Top

Circle the matching vowel sounds.

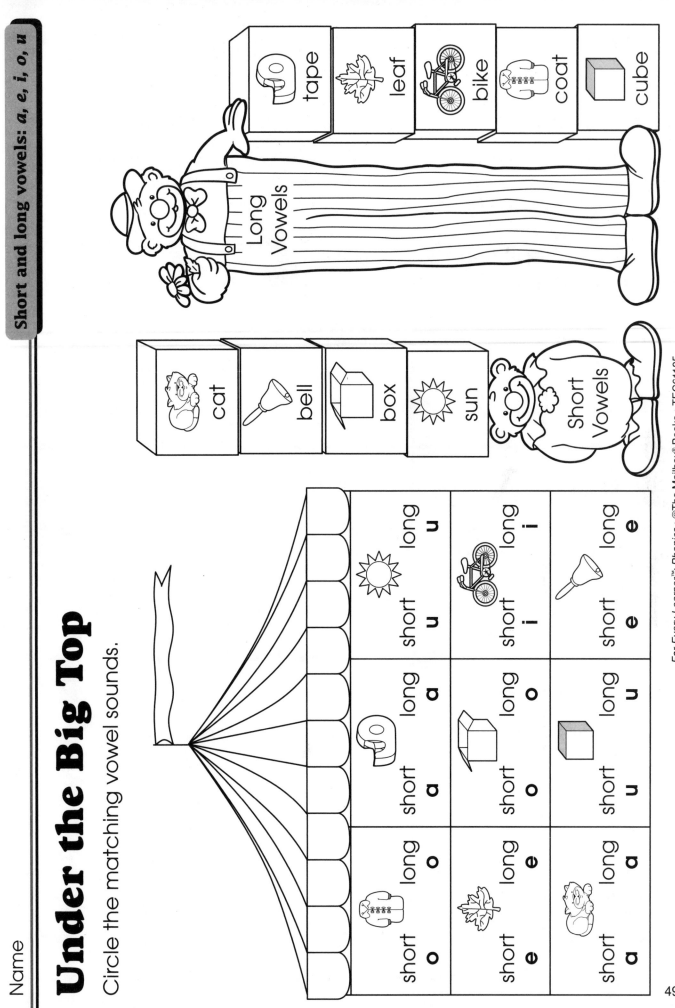

Long Vowels

tape

leaf

bike

coat

cube

Short Vowels

cat

bell

box

sun

short / long **o**	short / long **a**	short / long **u**
short / long **e**	short / long **o**	short / long **i**
short / long **a**	short / long **u**	short / long **e**

49

Missing Shoes

(Pages 50 and 51)

1. Cut out the cards below and stack them.
2. Name the picture on a card. Find the matching word on your other page.
3. Color the word's space by the code.
4. Repeat Steps 2 and 3 until all the cards have been used.

For Every Learner™: Phonics • ©The Mailbox® Books • TEC61185

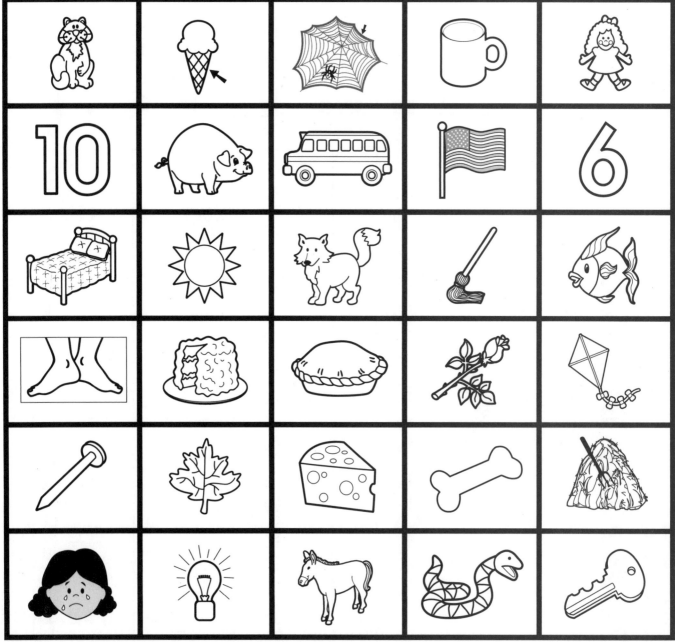

Missing Shoes

Color Code
Short vowel — orange
Long vowel — purple

feet	cake	pie	rose	cat
kite	web	mug	nail	cone
doll	leaf	ten	pig	bus
cry	flag	cheese	bone	hay
six	bed	sun	fox	mop
light	mule	snake	key	fish

For Every Learner™: Phonics • ©The Mailbox® Books • TEC61185

Clowning Around

Write the name of each picture on the matching line.

	Short **a**	Long **a**
	_____	_____
	Short **e**	Long **e**
	_____	_____
	Short **i**	Long **i**
	_____	_____
	Short **o**	Long **o**
	_____	_____
	Short **u**	Long **u**
	_____	_____

Finding Fish

1. Cut out the cards.
2. Glue the fish cards to the top of another sheet of paper.
3. Sort the other cards by word family.
4. Glue each set below the matching fish.

For Every Learner™: *Phonics* • ©The Mailbox® Books • TEC61185

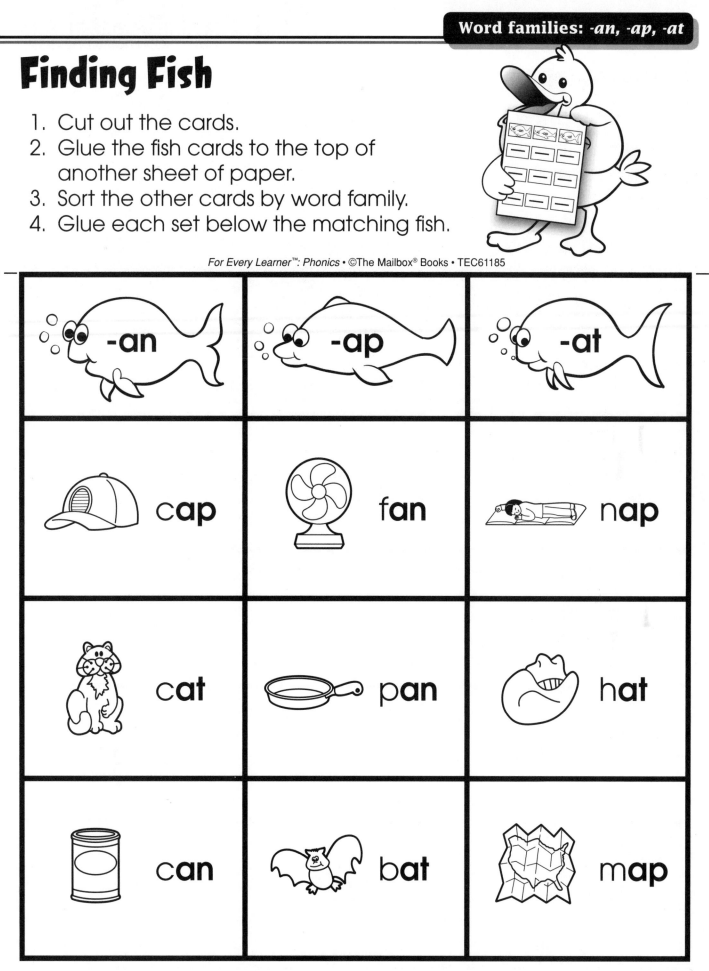

Boat Race
(Pages 54 and 55)

1. Cut out the cards below.
2. Take a card.
3. Write the word in the matching word family row on your other page.
4. Repeat Steps 2 and 3 for each card.
5. Color the boat for the row that reaches Finish first.

For Every Learner™: Phonics • ©The Mailbox® Books • TEC61185

cat	lap	hat
clap	ran	nap
that	plan	snap
than	mat	fan

Name

Boat Race

Finish

-an

-ap

-at

For Every Learner™: Phonics • ©The Mailbox® Books • TEC61185

Note to the teacher: Use with "Boat Race" on page 54.

Lots to Unload

Make words.
Use the letters and word families.
Cross out the letters you use.

-an

⨯m	p
g	th
c	f
h	pl

-ap

c	fl
m	b
sn	f
n	g

-at

d	f
c	th
m	h
j	ch

<u> man </u>

_____   _____   _____

_____   _____   _____

_____   _____   _____

_____   _____   _____

For Every Learner™: Phonics • ©The Mailbox® Books • TEC61185

Slow Swimmers

Write the word family to complete each word.

-ell

y _____

w _____

b _____

-et

v _____

n _____

j _____

-ock

s _____

l _____

r _____

-og

l _____

d _____

fr _____

Colorful Creature

Color by the code.

Color Code

-**ell**—green   -**ock**—red
-**et**—yellow   -**og**—blue

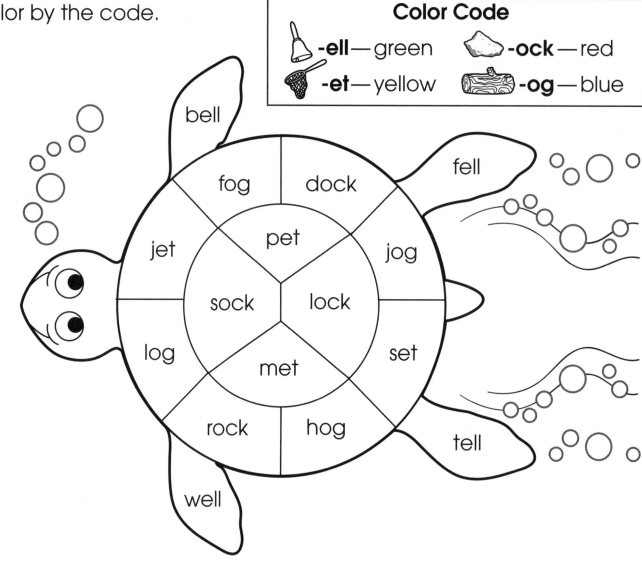

Write each word under its matching word family.

-ell	**-et**	**-ock**	**-og**
_____	_____	_____	_____
_____	_____	_____	_____
_____	_____	_____	_____
_____	_____	_____	_____

    For Every Learner™: *Phonics* • ©The Mailbox® Books • TEC61185

Terrific Turtles
(Pages 59 and 60)

1. Cut out the cards.
2. Sort the cards by word family.
3. Glue each set on a box on your other page.
4. Write the word family above each set.

For Every Learner™: Phonics • ©The Mailbox® Books • TEC61185

bell	jog	rock	wet
hog	met	fell	dog
clock	well	pet	dock
jet	sock	frog	tell

Terrific Turtles

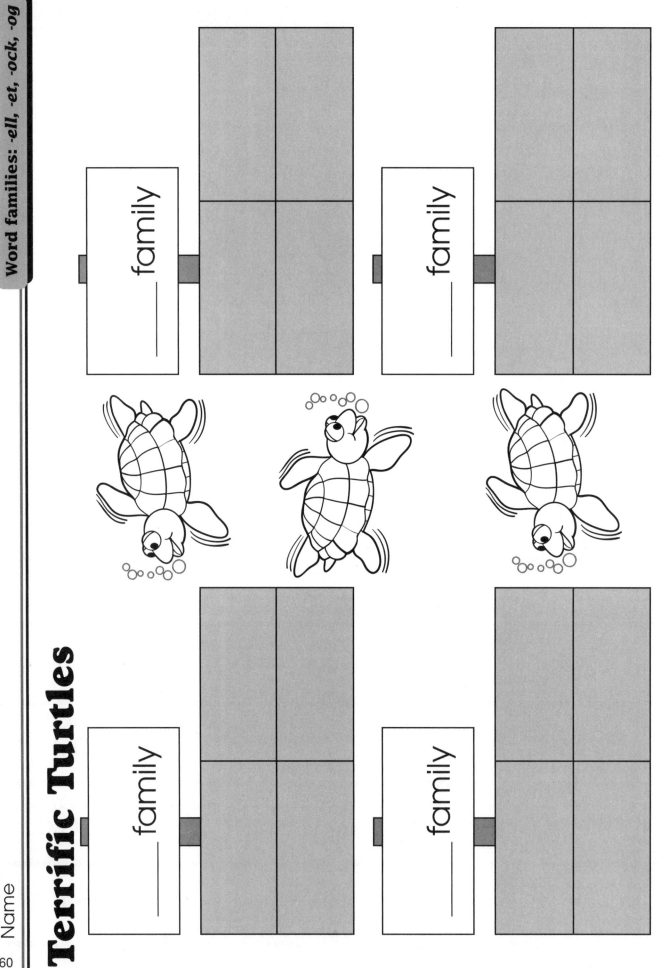

_____ family

_____ family

_____ family

_____ family

Balancing Act

1. Cut out the puzzle pieces. Mix them up.
2. Sort the cards by word family.
3. Put each set together to make a puzzle.
4. Glue the four puzzles on another sheet of paper.

For Every Learner™: Phonics • ©The Mailbox® Books • TEC61185

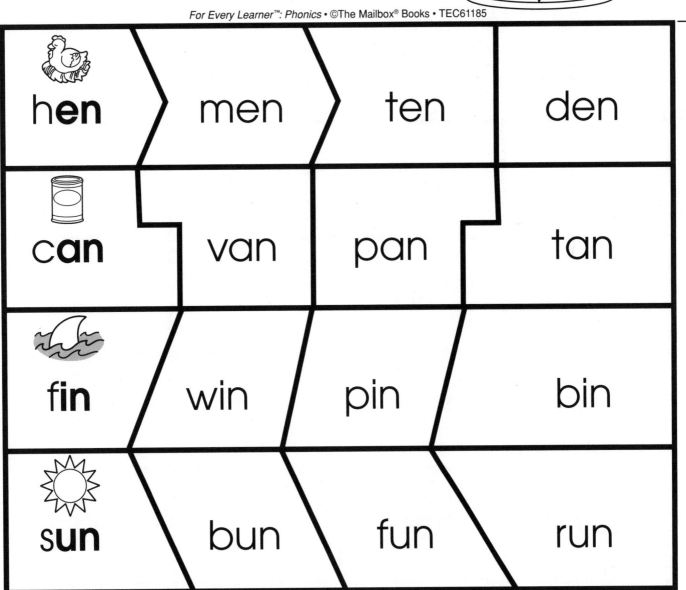

h**en**	men	ten	den
c**an**	van	pan	tan
f**in**	win	pin	bin
s**un**	bun	fun	run

On the Tightrope
(Pages 62 and 63)

1. Cut out the cards and stack them.
2. Read the word on a card. Name its word family.
3. Write the word in the matching row on your other page.
4. Repeat Steps 2 and 3 until all the cards have been used.

For Every Learner™: *Phonics* • ©The Mailbox® Books • TEC61185

can	hen	man	fin
men	bin	ten	pin
bun	fan	win	fun
run	pen	sun	pan

Name

On the Tightrope

-an _____ _____ _____

-en _____ _____ _____

-in _____ _____ _____

-un _____ _____ _____

For Every Learner™: *Phonics* • ©The Mailbox® Books • TEC61185

Note to the teacher: Use with "On the Tightrope" on page 62.

63

Slippin' and Slidin'

Use the letters or blends and the word families
   to make words.
Cross out the letters you use.

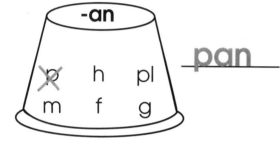

-an

~~p~~   h   pl
m   f   g

pan _____ _____ _____ _____

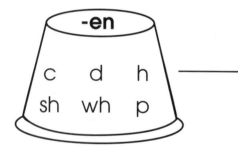

-en

c   d   h
sh   wh   p

_____ _____ _____ _____

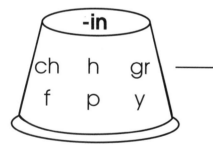

-in

ch   h   gr
f   p   y

_____ _____ _____ _____ _____

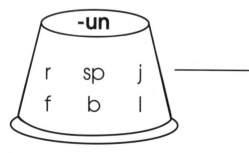

-un

r   sp   j
f   b   l

_____ _____ _____ _____

Frogs on Logs

Read the words in each word family.
Color to show the word in each puzzle.

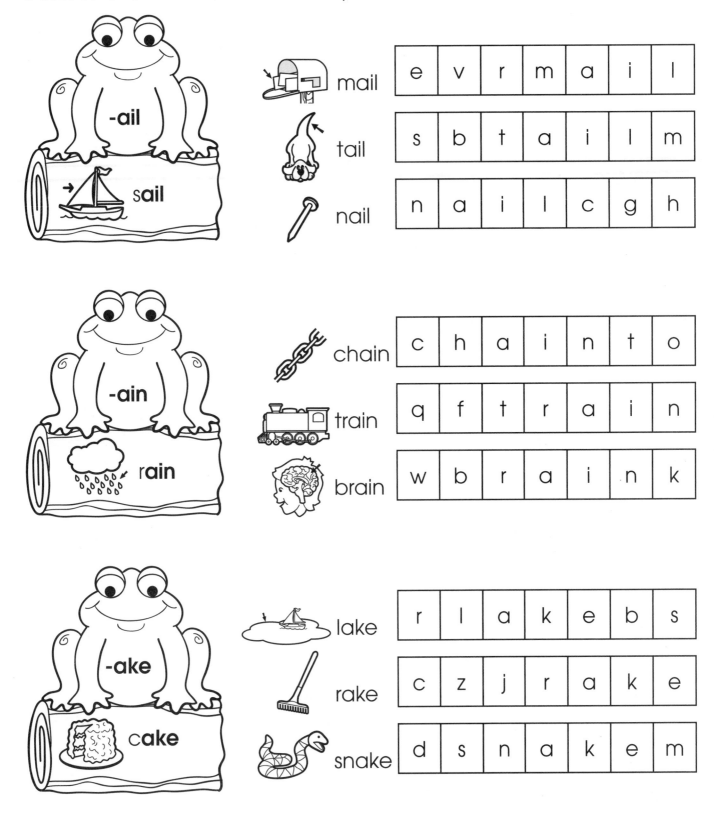

mail

| e | v | r | m | a | i | l |

tail

| s | b | t | a | i | l | m |

nail

| n | a | i | l | c | g | h |

chain

| c | h | a | i | n | t | o |

train

| q | f | t | r | a | i | n |

brain

| w | b | r | a | i | n | k |

lake

| r | l | a | k | e | b | s |

rake

| c | z | j | r | a | k | e |

snake

| d | s | n | a | k | e | m |

Rest Time

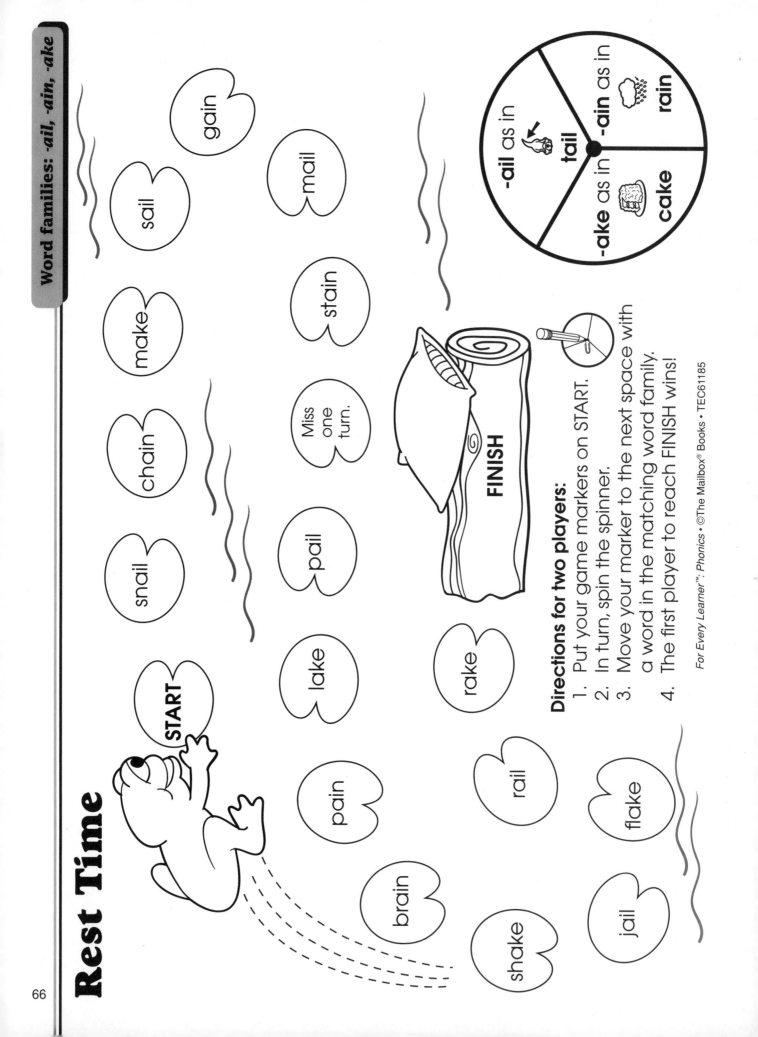

gain

sail

mail

make

stain

chain

Miss one turn.

snail

pail

FINISH

lake

rake

START

pain

rail

brain

flake

shake

jail

-ail as in tail

-ain as in rain

-ake as in cake

Directions for two players:
1. Put your game markers on START.
2. In turn, spin the spinner.
3. Move your marker to the next space with a word in the matching word family.
4. The first player to reach FINISH wins!

For Every Learner™: *Phonics* • ©The Mailbox® Books • TEC61185

Happy Hoppers!

(Pages 67 and 68)

1. Cut out the cards below.
2. Put a frog card in front of a log card. If they make a word, write it on the matching pond on your other page. Repeat with each frog card.
3. Repeat Step 2 with each log card.

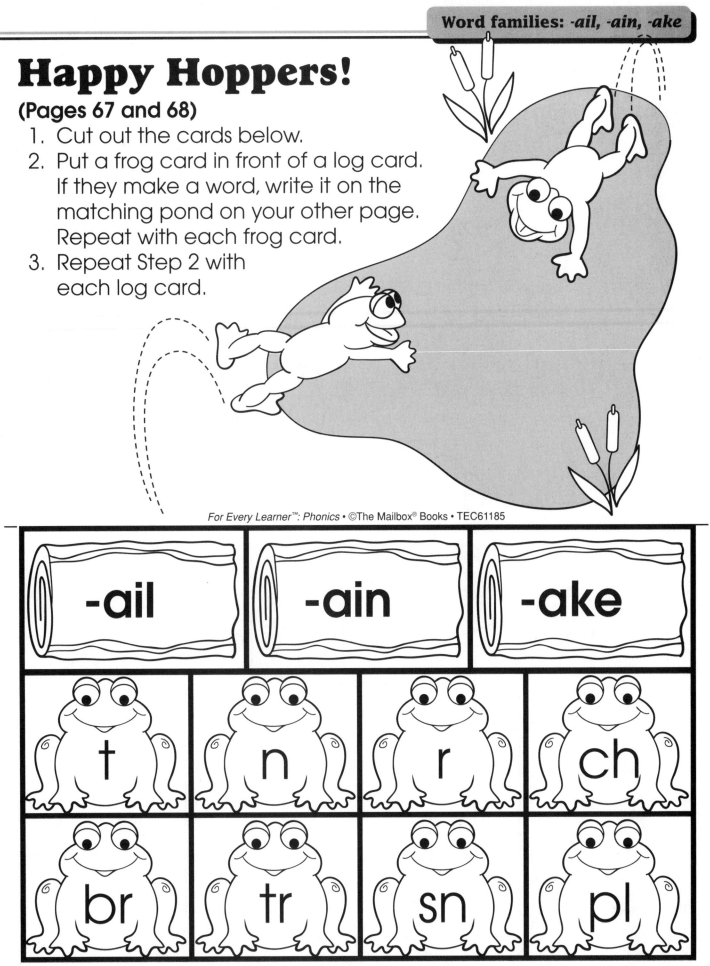

For Every Learner™: Phonics • ©The Mailbox® Books • TEC61185

-ail

-ain

-ake

t

n

r

ch

br

tr

sn

pl

Happy Hoppers!

-ain

-ail

-ake

For Every Learner™: Phonics • ©The Mailbox® Books • TEC61185

Note to the teacher: Use with "Happy Hoppers!" on page 67.

Bookmarks

(Pages 69 and 70)

1. Cut out the puzzle pieces. Mix them up.
2. Match each picture to its word.
3. Glue each puzzle under the matching word family on your other page.

For Every Learner™: Phonics • ©The Mailbox® Books • TEC61185

n**ight**

m**eat**

g**oat**

wh**eat**

b**oat**

r**ight**

c**oat**

l**ight**

h**eat**

70

Bookmarks

-oat

-ight

-eat

For Every Learner™: Phonics • ©The Mailbox® Books • TEC61185

Note to the teacher: Use with "Bookmarks" on page 69.

Name _____

Reading Zone

Color by the code.
Write each word under its matching word family.

Color Code
-eat — red
-ight — yellow
-oat — orange

Word families: -eat, -ight, -oat

neat	tight	sight	float	boat	seat
heat	right	might	coat	treat	throat

-eat

-ight

-oat

For Every Learner™: Phonics • ©The Mailbox® Books • TEC61185

Fun With Books

Circle the **-eat**, **-ight**, or **-oat** word family word(s) in each sentence. Write each word under its matching word family.

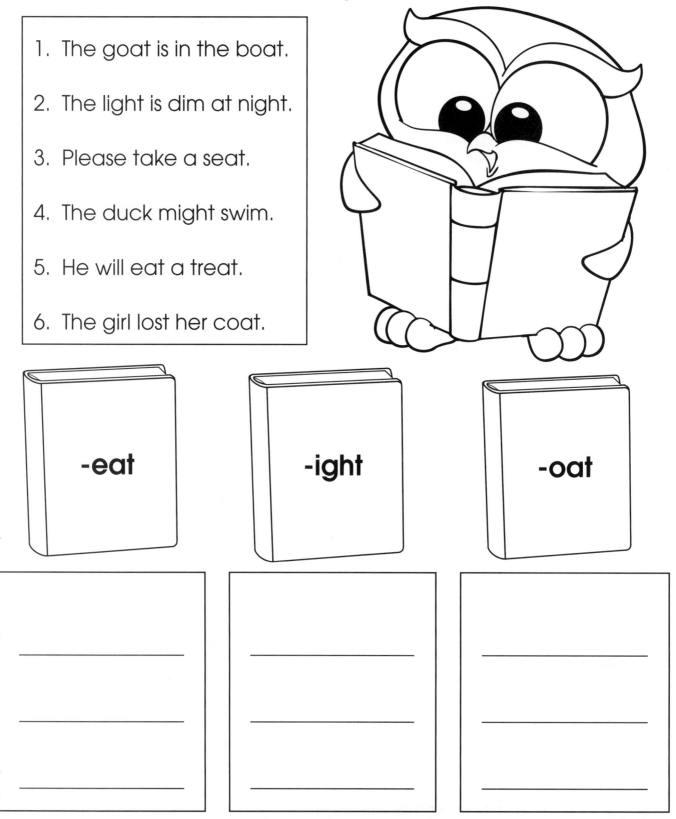

1. The goat is in the boat.

2. The light is dim at night.

3. Please take a seat.

4. The duck might swim.

5. He will eat a treat.

6. The girl lost her coat.

-eat

-ight

-oat

For Every Learner™: *Phonics* • ©The Mailbox® Books • TEC61185

Bugs! Bugs! Bugs!

1. Cut out the cards.
2. Glue each bug card along the left side of another sheet of paper.
3. Sort the cards by blends.
4. Glue each set next to the matching bug card.

For Every Learner™: Phonics • ©The Mailbox® Books • TEC61185

sk	**sp**	**st**	**sm**
stick	skunk	sponge	spill
smell	stem	steak	smoke
smile	spider	skirt	skate

Moving Along

(Pages 74 and 75)

1. Cut out the cards below.
2. Name each picture on your other page.
3. Glue on a blend to complete each word.
4. Write each word on the matching line.

sk	sk	sk	sm	sm
sm	sp	sp	st	st

Moving Along

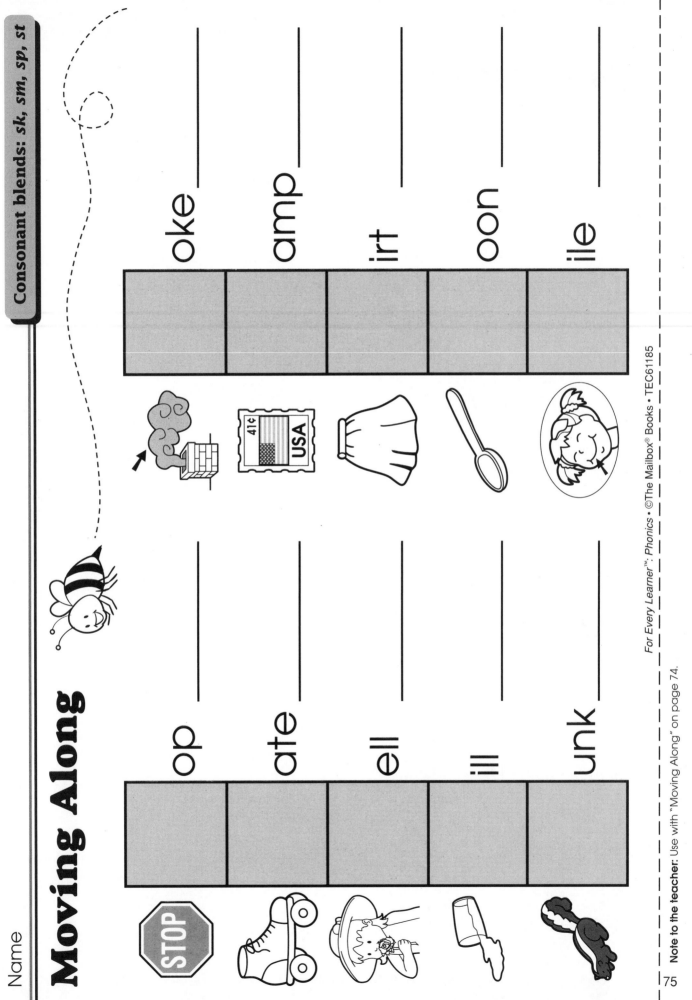

____ oke

____ amp

____ irt

____ oon

____ ile

____ op

____ ate

____ ell

____ ill

____ unk

For Every Learner™: Phonics • ©The Mailbox® Books • TEC61185

Note to the teacher: Use with "Moving Along" on page 74.

Super Thinker

Read.
Write each new word.

sk   sm
sp   st

1. change **bell** to

2. change **trunk** to

3. change **moon** to

4. change **plate** to

5. change **lip** to

6. change **pool** to

7. change **well** to

8. change **joke** to

9. change **car** to

10. change **shirt** to

For Every Learner™: Phonics • ©The Mailbox® Books • TEC61185

Housework Helpers

(Pages 77 and 78)

1. Cut out the cards.
2. Put a dot of glue on each • on your other page.
3. Glue each card to a picture with the same digraph.

For Every Learner™: Phonics • ©The Mailbox® Books • TEC61185

ch	sh	th	wh
ch	sh	th	wh
ch	sh	th	wh

Housework Helpers

chair	**sh**ip	**th**ink	**sh**oe
wheel	**th**umb	**ch**eese	**wh**istle
chain	**wh**ale	**th**irteen	**sh**irt

For Every Learner™: Phonics • ©The Mailbox® Books • TEC61185

Note to the teacher: Use with "Housework Helpers" on page 77.

Dishwashing Duty

1. Write **ch, sh, th,** or **wh** to finish each word below.
2. Cut out the cards.
3. Sort the cards by digraph.
4. Glue each set together on another sheet of paper.
5. Label each set with its digraph.

For Every Learner™: Phonics • ©The Mailbox® Books • TEC61185

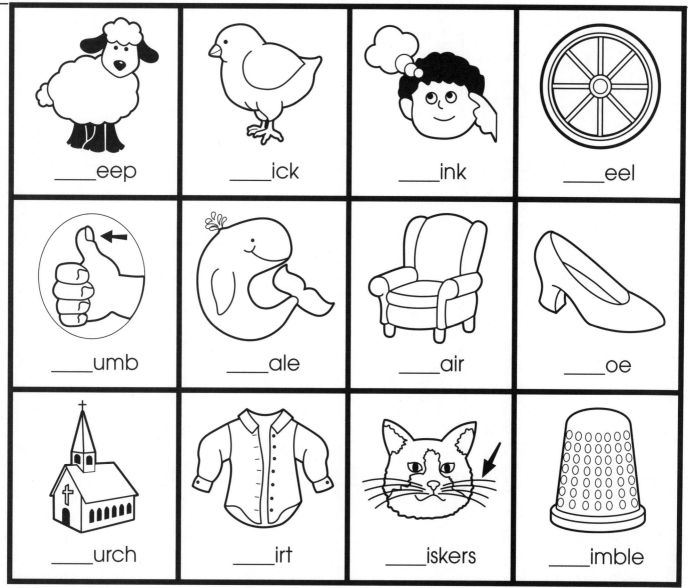

___eep

___ick

___ink

___eel

___umb

___ale

___air

___oe

___urch

___irt

___iskers

___imble

80 Name

Make It Up

Color by the code.

Color Code

ch—blue   sh—red   wh—green
th—orange

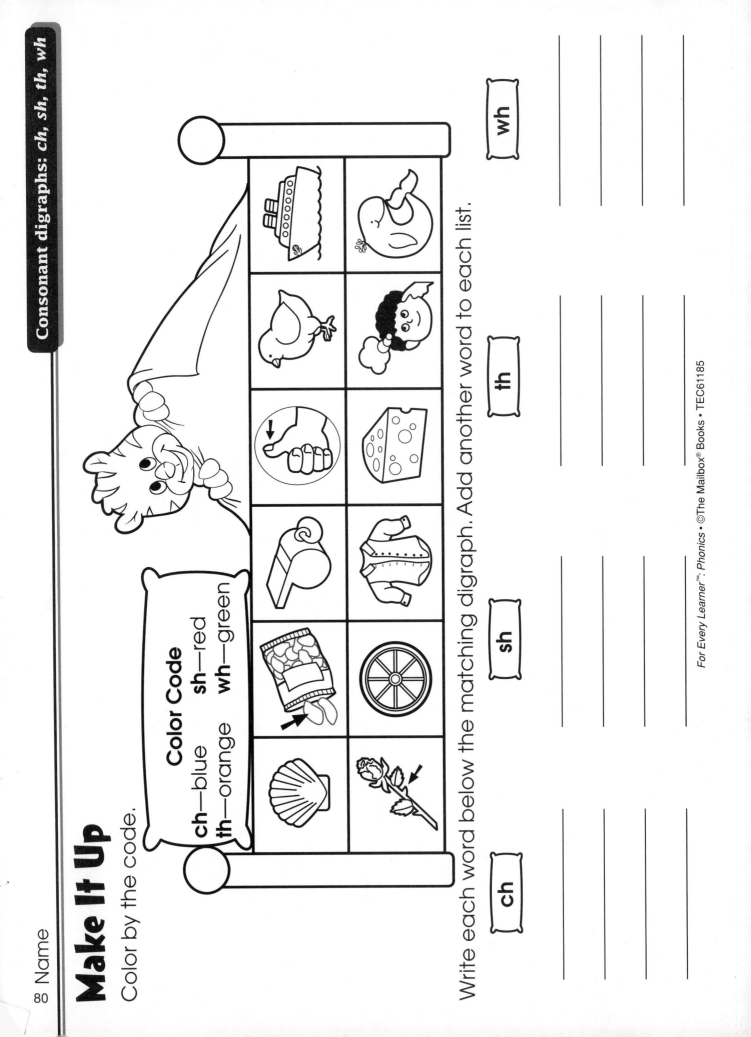

Write each word below the matching digraph. Add another word to each list.

ch	sh	th	wh